The Princess and th

Evelyn E. Smith

Alpha Editions

This edition published in 2024

ISBN 9789362099105

Design and Setting By

Alpha Editions
www.alphaedis.com

Email - info@alphaedis.com

As per information held with us this book is in Public Domain.
This book is a reproduction of an important historical work.
Alpha Editions uses the best technology to reproduce historical work
in the same manner it was first published to preserve its original nature.
Any marks or number seen are left intentionally to preserve.

The Princess and the Physicist

Zen the Terrible lay quiescent in the secret retreat which housed his corporeal being, all the aspects of his personality wallowing in the luxury of a day off. How glad he was that he'd had the forethought to stipulate a weekly holiday for himself when first this godhood had been thrust upon him, hundreds of centuries before. He'd accepted the perquisites of divinity with pleasure then. It was some little time before he discovered its drawbacks, and by then it was too late; he had become the established church.

All the aspects of his personality rested ... save one, that is. And that one, stretching out an impalpable tendril of curiosity, brought back to his total consciousness the news that a spaceship from Earth had arrived when no ship from Earth was due.

So what? the total consciousness asked lazily of itself. *Probably they have a large out-of-season order for hajench. My hajench going to provide salad bowls for barbarians!*

When, twenty years previously, the Earthmen had come back to their colony on Uxen after a lapse of thousands of years, Zen had been hopeful that they would take some of the Divine Work off his hands. After all, since it was they who had originally established the colony, it should be their responsibility. But it seemed that all humans, not merely the Uxenach, were irresponsible. The Earthmen were interested only in trade and tribute. They even refused to believe in the existence of Zen, an attitude which he found extremely irritating to his ego.

True, Uxen prospered commercially to a mild extent after their return, for the local ceramics that had been developed in the long interval found wide acceptance throughout the Galaxy, particularly the low bowls which had hitherto been used only for burning incense before Zen the Formidable.

Now every two-bit planet offered hajench in its gift shops.

Culturally, though, Uxen had degenerated under the new Earth administration. No more criminals were thrown to the skwitch. Xwoosh lost its interest when new laws prohibited the ancient custom of executing the losing side after each game.

There was no tourist trade, for the planet was too far from the rest of the Galaxy. The commercial spaceships came only once every three months and left the same day. The two destroyers that "guarded" the planet arrived at rare intervals for fueling or repairs, but the crew never had anything to do with the Uxenach. Local ordinance forbade the maidens of Uxen to speak to the outlanders, and the outlanders were not interested in any of the other native products.

But the last commercial spaceship had departed less than three weeks before on its regular run, and this was not one of the guard ships.

Zen reluctantly conceded to himself that he would have to investigate this situation further, if he wanted to retain his reputation for omniscience. Sometimes, in an occasional moment of self-doubt, he wondered if he weren't too much of a perfectionist, but then he rejected the thought as self-sacrilege.

Zen dutifully intensified the beam of awareness and returned it to the audience chamber where the two strange Earthmen who had come on the ship were being ushered into the presence of the king by none other than Guj, the venerable prime minister himself.

"Gentlemen," Guj beamed, his long white beard vibrating in an excess of hospitality, "His Gracious Majesty will be delighted to receive you at once."

And crossing his wrists in the secular xa, he led the way to where Uxlu the Fifteenth was seated in full regalia upon his imposing golden, gem-encrusted throne.

Uxlu himself, Zen admitted grudgingly, was an imposing sight to anyone who didn't know the old yio. The years—for he was a scant decade younger than Guj—had merely lent dignity to his handsome features, and he was still tall and upright.

"Welcome, Earthlings, to Uxen," King Uxlu said in the sonorous tones of the practiced public speaker. "If there is aught we can do to advance your comfort whilst you sojourn on our little planet, you have but to speak."

He did not, Zen noted with approval, rashly promise that requests would necessarily be granted. Which was fine, because the god well knew who the carrier out of requests would be—Zen the Almighty, the All-Powerful, the All-Put-Upon....

"Thank you, Your Majesty," the older of the two scientists said. "We merely seek a retired spot in which to conduct our researches."

"Researches, eh?" the king repeated with warm interest. "Are you perhaps scientists?"

"Yes, Your Majesty." Every one of Zen's perceptors quivered expectantly. Earth science was banned on Uxen, with the result that its acquisition had become the golden dream of every Uxena, including, of course, their god.

The older scientist gave a stiff bow. "I am an anthropologist. My name is Kendrick, Professor Alpheus Kendrick. My assistant, Dr. Peter Hammond—" he indicated the tall young man with him—"is a physicist."

The king and the prime minister conferred together in whispers. Zen wished he could join them, but he couldn't materialize on that plane without incense, and he preferred his subjects not to know that he could be invisibly present, especially on his day off. Of course, his Immaterial Omnipresence was a part of the accepted dogma, but there is a big difference between accepting a concept on a basis of faith or of proven fact.

"Curious researches," the king said, emerging from the conference, "that require both physics *and* anthropology."

"Yes," said Kendrick. "They are rather involved at that." Peter Hammond shuffled his feet.

"Perhaps some of our technicians might be of assistance to you," the king suggested. "They may not have your science, but they are very adept with their hands...."

"Our researches are rather limited in scope," Kendrick assured him. "We can do everything needful quite adequately ourselves. All we need is a place in which to do it."

"You shall have our own second-best palace," the king said graciously. "It has both hot and cold water laid on, as well as central heating."

"We've brought along our own collapsible laboratory-dwelling," Kendrick explained. "We just want a spot to set it up."

Uxin sighed. "The royal parks are at your disposal. You will undoubtedly require servants?"

"We have a robot, thanks."

"A robot is a mechanical man who does all our housework," Hammond, more courteous than his superior, explained. Zen wondered how he could ever have felt a moment's uneasiness concerning these wonderful strangers.

"Zen will be interested to hear of this," the prime minister said cannily. He and the king nodded at one another.

"*Who* did you say?" Kendrick asked eagerly.

"Zen the Terrible," the king repeated, "Zen the All-Powerful, Zen the Encyclopedic. Surely you have heard of him?" he asked in some surprise. "He's Uxen's own particular, personal and private god, exclusive to our planet."

"Yes, yes, of course I've heard about him," Kendrick said, trembling with hardly repressed excitement.

What a correct attitude! Zen thought. *One rarely finds such religious respect among foreigners.*

"In fact, I've heard a great deal about him and I should like to know even more!" Kendrick spoke almost reverently.

"He *is* an extremely interesting divinity," the king replied complacently. "And if your robot cannot teleport or requires a hand with the heavy work, do not hesitate to call on Zen the Accommodating. We'll detail a priest to summon—"

"The robot manages very well all by itself, thank you," Kendrick said quickly.

In his hideaway, the material body of Zen breathed a vast multiple sigh of relief. He was getting to like these Earthmen more and more by the minute.

"Might I inquire," the king asked, "into the nature of your researches?"

"An investigation of the prevalent nuclear ritual beliefs on Uxen in relation to the over-all matrix of social culture, and we really must get along and see to the unloading of the ship. Good-by, Your Majesty ... Your Excellency." And Kendrick dragged his protesting aide off.

"If only," said the king, "I were still an absolute monarch, I would teach these Earthlings some manners." His face grew wistful. "Well I remember how my father would have those who crossed him torn apart by wild skwitch."

"If you did have the Earthlings torn apart by wild skwitch, Sire," Guj pointed out, "then you would certainly never be able to obtain any information from them."

Uxlu sighed. "I would merely have them torn apart a little—just enough so that they would answer a few civil questions." He sighed again. "And, supposing they did happen to—er—pass on, in the process, think of the tremendous lift to my ego. But nobody thinks of the king's ego any more these days."

No, things were not what they had been since the time the planet had been retrieved by the Earthlings. They had not communicated with Uxen for so many hundreds of years, they had explained, because, after a more than ordinarily disastrous war, they had lost the secret of space travel for centuries.

Now, wanting to make amends for those long years of neglect, they immediately provided that the Earth language and the Earth income tax become mandatory upon Uxen. The language was taught by recordings. Since the Uxenach were a highly intelligent people, they had all learned it quickly and forgotten most of their native tongue except for a few untranslatable concepts.

"Must be a new secret atomic weapon they're working on," Uxlu decided. "Why else should they come to such a remote corner of the Galaxy? And you will recall that the older one—Kendrick—said something about nuclear beliefs. If only we could discover what it is, secure it for ourselves, perhaps we could defeat the Earthmen, drive them away—" he sighed for the third time that morning—"and rule the planet ourselves."

Just then the crown princess Iximi entered the throne room. Iximi really lived up to her title of Most Fair and Exalted, for centuries of selective breeding under which the kings of Uxen had seized the loveliest women of the planet for their wives had resulted in an outstanding pulchritude. Her hair was as golden as the ripe fruit that bent the boughs of the iolo tree, and her eyes were bluer than the uriz stones on the belt girdling her slender waist. Reproductions of the famous portrait of her which hung in the great hall of the palace were very popular on calendars.

"My father grieves," she observed, making the secular xa. "Pray tell your unworthy daughter what sorrow racks your noble bosom."

"Uxen is a backwash," her father mourned. "A planet forgotten, while the rest of the Galaxy goes by. Our ego has reached its nadir."

"Why did you let yourself be conquered?" the princess retorted scornfully. "Ah, had I been old enough to speak then, matters would be very different today!" Although she seemed too beautiful to be endowed with brains, Iximi had been graduated from the Royal University with high honors.

Zen the Erudite was particularly fond of her, for she had been his best student in Advanced Theology. She was, moreover, an ardent patriot and leader of the underground Moolai (free) Uxen movement, with which Zen was more or less in sympathy, since he felt Uxen belonged to him and not to the Earthlings. After all, he had been there first.

"*Let* ourselves be conquered!" Her father's voice rose to a squeak. "*Let* ourselves! Nobody asked us—we *were* conquered."

"True, but we could at least have essayed our strength against the conquerors instead of capitulating like yioch. We could have fought to the last man!"

"A woman is always ready to fight to the last man," Guj commented.

"Did you hear that, ancient and revered parent! He called me, a princess of the blood, a—a woman!"

"We are all equal before Zen," Guj said sententiously, making the high xa.

"Praise Zen," Uxlu and Iximi chanted perfunctorily, bowing low.

Iximi, still angry, ordered Guj—who was also high priest—to start services. Kindling the incense in the hajen, he began the chant.

Of course it was his holiday, but Zen couldn't resist the appeal of the incense. Besides he was there anyway, so it was really no trouble, *no trouble*, he thought, greedily sniffing the delicious aroma, *at all*. He materialized a head with seven nostrils so that he was able to inhale the incense in one delectable gulp. Then, "No prayers answered on Thursday," he said, and disappeared. That would show them!

"Drat Zen and his days off!" The princess was in a fury. "Very well, we'll manage without Zen the Spiteful. Now, precisely what is troubling you, worthy and undeservedly Honored Parent?"

"Those two scientists who arrived from Earth. Didn't you meet them when you came in?"

"No, Respected Father," she said, sitting on the arm of the throne. "I must have just missed them. What are they like?"

He told her what they were like in terms not even a monarch should use before his daughter. "And these squuch," he concluded, "are undoubtedly working on a secret weapon. If we had it, we could free Uxen."

"Moolai Uxen!" the princess shouted, standing up. "My friends, must we continue to submit to the yoke of the tyrant? Arise. Smite the...."

"Anyone," said Guj, "can make a speech."

The princess sat on the steps of the throne and pondered. "Obviously we must introduce a spy into their household to learn their science and turn it to our advantage."

"They are very careful, those Earthlings," Guj informed her superciliously. "It is obvious that they do not intend to let any of us come near them."

The princess gave a knowing smile. "But they undoubtedly will need at least one menial to care for their dwelling. I shall be that menial. I, Iximi, will so demean myself for the sake of my planet! Moolai Uxen!"

"You cannot do it, Iximi," her father said, distressed. "You must not defile yourself so. I will not hear of it!"

"And besides," Guj interposed, "they will need no servants. All their housework is to be done by their robot—a mechanical man that performs all menial duties. And you, Your Royal Highness, could not plausibly disguise yourself as a machine."

"No-o-o-o, I expect not." The princess hugged the rosy knees revealed by her brief tunic and thought aloud, "But ... just ... supposing ... something ... went wrong with the robot.... They do not possess another?"

"They referred only to one, Highness," Guj replied reluctantly. "But they may have the parts with which to construct another."

"Nonetheless, it is well worth the attempt," the princess declared. "You will cast a spell on the robot, Guj, so that it stops."

He sighed. "Very well, Your Highness; I suppose I could manage that!"

Making the secular xa, he left the royal pair. Outside, his voice could be heard bellowing in the anteroom, "Has any one of you squuch seen my pliers?"

"There is no need for worry, Venerated Ancestor," the princess assured the monarch. "All-Helpful Zen will aid me with my tasks."

Far away in his arcane retreat, the divinity groaned to himself.

Another aspect of Zen's personality followed the two Earthmen as they left the palace to supervise the erection of their prefab by the crew of the spaceship in one of the Royal Parks. A vast crowd of Uxenach gathered to watch the novelty, and among them there presently appeared a sinister-looking old man with a red beard, whom Zen the Pansophic had no difficulty in recognizing as the prime minister, heavily disguised. Of course it would have been no trouble for Zen to carry out Guj's mission for him, but he believed in self-help—especially on Thursdays.

"You certainly fixed us up fine!" Hammond muttered disrespectfully to the professor. "You should've told the king we were inventing a vacuum cleaner or something. Now they'll just be more curious than ever.... And I still don't see why you refused the priest. Seems to me he'd be just what you needed."

"Yes, and the first to catch on to why we're here. We mustn't antagonize the natives; these closed groups are so apt to resent any investigation into their mythos."

"If it's all mythical, why do you need a scientist then?"

"A physical scientist, you mean," Kendrick said austerely. "For anthropology is a science, too, you know."

Peter snorted.

"Some Earthmen claim actually to have seen these alleged manifestations," Kendrick went on to explain, "in which case there must be some kind of mechanical trickery involved—which is where you come in. Of course I would have preferred an engineer to help me, but you were all I could get from the government."

"And you wouldn't have got me either, if the Minister of Science didn't have it in for me!" Peter said irately. "I'm far too good for this piddling little job, and you know it. If it weren't for envy in high places—"

"Better watch out," the professor warned, "or the Minister might decide you're too good for science altogether, and you'll be switched to a position more in keeping with your talents—say, as a Refuse Removal Agent."

And what is wrong with the honored art of Refuse Removal? Zen wondered. There were a lot of mystifying things about these Earthmen.

The scientists' quaint little edifice was finally set up, and the spaceship took its departure. It was only then that the Earthmen discovered that something they called cigarettes couldn't be found in the welter of packages, and that the robot wouldn't cook dinner or, in fact, do anything. *Good old Guj*, Zen thought.

"I can't figure out what's gone wrong," Peter complained, as he finished putting the mechanical man together again. "Everything seems to be all right, and yet the damned thing won't function."

"Looks as if we'll have to do the housework ourselves, confound it!"

"Uh-uh," Peter said. "You can, but not me. The Earth government put me under your orders so far as this project is concerned, sir, but I'm not supposed to do anything degrading, sir, and menial work is classified as just that, sir, so—"

"All right, all *right*!" Kendrick said. "Though it seems to me if *I'm* willing to do it, *you* should have no objection."

"It's your project, sir. I gathered from the king, though," Peter added more helpfully, "that some of the natives still do menial labor themselves."

"How disgusting that there should still be a planet so backward that human beings should be forced to do humiliating tasks," Kendrick said.

You don't know the half of it, either, Zen thought, shocked all the way back to his physical being. It had never occurred to him that the functions of gods on other planets might be different than on Uxen ... unless the Earthlings failed to pay reverence to their own gods, which seemed unlikely in view of the respectful way with which Professor Kendrick had greeted the mention of Zen's Awe-Inspiring Name. Then Refuse Removal was not necessarily a divine prerogative.

Those first colonists were very clever, Zen thought bitterly, *sweet-talking me into becoming a god and doing all their dirty work. I was happy here as the Only Inhabitant; why did I ever let those interlopers involve me in Theolatry? But I can't quit now. The Uxenach need Me ... and I need incense; I'm fettered by my own weakness. Still, I have the glimmerings of an idea....*

"Oh, how much could a half-witted menial find out?" Peter demanded. "Remember, it's either a native servant, sir, or you do the housework yourself."

"All right," Kendrick agreed gloomily. "We'll try one of the natives."

So the next day, still attended by the Unseen Presence of Zen, they sought audience with the prime minister.

"Welcome, Earthmen, to the humble apartments of His Majesty's most unimportant subject," Guj greeted them, making a very small xa as he led them into the largest reception room.

Kendrick absently ran his finger over the undercarving of a small gold table. "Look, no dust," he whispered. "Must have excellent help here."

Zen couldn't help preening just a bit. At least he did his work well; no one could gainsay that.

"Your desire," Guj went on, apparently anxious to get to the point, "is my command. Would you like a rojh of dancing girls to perform before you or—?"

"The king said something yesterday about servants being available," Kendrick interrupted. "And our robot seems to have broken down. Could you tell us where we could get someone to do our housework?"

An expression of vivid pleasure illuminated the prime minister's venerable countenance. "By fortunate chance, gentlemen, a small lot of maids is to be auctioned off at a village very near the Imperial City tomorrow. I should be delighted to escort you there personally."

"Auctioned?" Kendrick repeated. "You mean they *sell* servants here?"

Guj raised his snowy eyebrows. "Sold? Certainly not; they are leased for two years apiece. After all, if you have no lease, what guarantee do you have that your servants will stay after you have trained them? None whatsoever."

When the two scientists had gone, Iximi emerged from behind a bright-colored tapestry depicting Zen in seven hundred and fifty-three of his Attributes.

"The younger one is not at all bad-looking," she commented, patting her hair into place. "I do like big blond men. Perhaps my task will not be as unpleasant as I fancied."

Guj stroked his beard. "How do you know the Earthlings will select you, Your Highness? Many other maids will be auctioned off at the same time."

The princess stiffened angrily. "They'll pick me or they'll never leave Uxen alive and you, Your Excellency, would not outlive them."

Although it meant he had to overwork the other aspects of his multiple personality, Zen kept one free so that the next day he could join the Earthmen—in spirit, that was—on their excursion in search of a menial.

"If, as an anthropologist, you are interested in local folkways, Professor," Guj remarked graciously, as he and the scientists piled into a scarlet, boat-shaped vehicle, "you will find much to attract your attention in this quaint little planet of ours."

"Are the eyes painted on front of the car to ward off demons?" Kendrick asked.

"Car? Oh, you mean the yio!" Guj patted the forepart of the vehicle. It purred and fluttered long eyelashes. "We breed an especially bouncy strain with seats; they're so much more comfortable, you know."

"You mean this is a *live* animal?"

Guj nodded apologetically. "Of course it does not go very fast. Now if we had the atomic power drive, such as your spaceships have—"

"You'd shoot right off into space," Hammond assured him.

"Speed," said Kendrick, "is the curse of modern civilization. Be glad you still retain some of the old-fashioned graces here on Uxen. You see," he whispered to his assistant, "a clear case of magico-religious culture-freezing, resulting in a static society unable to advance itself, comes of its implicit reliance upon the powers of an omnipotent deity."

Zen took some time to figure this out. *But that's right!* he concluded, in surprise.

"I thought your god teleported things?" Peter asked Guj. "How come he doesn't teleport you around, if you're in such a hurry to go places?"

Kendrick glared at him. "Please remember that I'm the anthropologist," he hissed. "You have got to know how to describe the Transcendental Personality with the proper respect."

"We don't have Zen teleport animate objects," the prime minister explained affably. "Or even inanimate ones if they are fragile. For He tends to lose His Temper sometimes when He feels that He is overworked—" *Feels, indeed!* Zen said to himself—"and throws things about. We cannot reprove Him for His misbehavior. After all, a god is a god."

"The apparent irreverence," Kendrick explained in an undertone, "undoubtedly signifies that he is dealing with ancillary or, perhaps, peripheral religious beliefs. I must make a note of them." He did so.

By the time the royal yio had arrived at the village where the planetary auctions for domestics were held, the maids were already arranged in a row on the platform. Most were depressingly plain creatures and dressed in thick sacklike tunics. Among them, the graceful form of Iximi was conspicuous, clad in a garment similar in cut but fashioned of translucent gauze almost as blue as her eyes.

Peter straightened his tie and assumed a much more cheerful expression. "Let's rent *that one!*" he exclaimed, pointing to the princess.

"Nonsense!" Kendrick told him. "In the first place, she is obviously the most expensive model. Secondly, she would be too distracting for you. And, finally, a pretty girl is never as good a worker as a plain.... We'll take that one." The professor pointed to the dumpiest and oldest of the women. "How much should I offer to start, Your Excellency? No sense beginning the bidding too high. We Earthmen aren't made of money, in spite of what the rest of the Galaxy seems to think."

"A hundred credits is standard," Guj murmured. "However, sir, there is one problem—have you considered how you are going to communicate with your maid?"

"Communicate? Are they mutes?"

"No, but very few of these women speak Earth." A look of surprise flitted over the faces of the servants, vanishing as her royal highness glared at them.

Kendrick pursed thin lips. "I was under the impression that the Earth language was mandatory on Uxen."

"Oh, it is; it is, indeed!" Guj said hastily. "However, it is so hard to teach these backward peasants new ways." One of the backward peasants gave a loud sniff, which changed to a squeal as she was honored with a pinch from the hand of royalty. "But you will not betray us? We are making rapid advances and before long we hope to make Earth universal."

"Of course we won't," Peter put in, before Kendrick had a chance to reply. "What's more, I don't see why the Uxenians shouldn't be allowed to speak their own language."

The princess gave him a dazzling smile. "Moolai Uxen! We must not allow the beautiful Uxulk tongue to fall into desuetude. Bring back our lovely language!"

Guj gestured desperately. She tossed her head, but stopped.

"Please, Kendrick," Peter begged, "we've got to buy that one!"

"Certainly not. You can see she's a troublemaker. Do you speak Earth?" the professor demanded of the maid he had chosen.

"No speak," she replied.

Peter tugged at his superior's sleeve. "That one speaks Earth."

Kendrick shook him off. "Do you speak Earth?" he demanded of the second oldest and ugliest. She shook her head. The others went through the same procedure.

"It looks," Peter said, grinning, "as if we'll have to take mine."

"I suppose so," Kendrick agreed gloomily, "but somehow I feel no good will come of this."

Zen wondered whether Earthmen had powers of precognition.

No one bid against them, so they took a two-year lease on the crown princess for the very reasonable price of a hundred credits, and drove her home with them.

Iximi gazed at the little prefab with disfavor. "But why are we halting outside this gluu hutch, masters?"

Guj cleared his throat. "Sirs, I wish you joy." He made the secular xa. "Should you ever be in need again, do not hesitate to get in touch with me at the palace." And, climbing into the yio, he was off.

The others entered the small dwelling. "That little trip certainly gave me an appetite," Kendrick said, rubbing his hands together. "Iximi, you had better start lunch right away. This is the kitchen."

Iximi gazed around the cubicle with disfavor. "Truly it is not much," she observed. "However, masters, if you will leave me, I shall endeavor to do my poor best."

"Let me show you—" Peter began, but Kendrick interrupted.

"Leave the girl alone, Hammond. She must be able to cook, if she's a professional servant. We've wasted the whole morning as it is; maybe we can get something done before lunch."

Iximi closed the door, got out her portable altar—all members of the royal family were qualified members of the priesthood, though they seldom practiced—and in a low voice, for the door and walls were thin, summoned Zen the All-Capable.

The god sighed as he materialized his head. "I might have known you would require Me. What is your will, oh Most Fair?"

"I have been ordered to prepare the strangers' midday repast, oh Puissant One, and I know not what to do with all this ukh, which they assure me is their food." And she pointed scornfully to the cans and jars and packages.

"How should *I* know then?" Zen asked unguardedly.

The princess looked at him. "Surely Zen the All-Knowing jests?"

- 15 -

"Er—yes. Merely having My Bit of Fun, you know." He hastily inspected the exterior of the alleged foods. "There appear to be legends inscribed upon the containers. Perchance, were we to read them, they might give a clue as to their contents."

"Oh, Omniscent One," the princess exclaimed, "truly You are Wise and Sapient indeed, and it is I who was the fool to have doubted for so much as an instant."

"Oh you doubted, did you?" Terrible Zen frowned terribly. "Well, see that it doesn't happen again." He had no intention of losing his divine authority at this stage of the game.

"Your Will is mine, All-Wise One. And I think You had best materialize a few pair of arms as well as Your August and Awe-inspiring Countenance, for there is much work to be done."

Since the partitions were thin, Zen and the princess could hear most of the conversation in the main room. "... First thing to do," Kendrick's voice remarked, "is find out whether we're permitted to attend one of their religious ceremonies, where Zen is said to manifest himself actually and not, it is contended, just symbolically...."

"The stove is here, Almighty," the princess suggested, "not against the door where you are pressing Your Divine Ear."

"Shhh. What I hear is fraught with import for the future of the planet. Moolai Uxen."

"Moolai Uxen," the princess replied automatically.

"... I wonder how hard it'll be to crash the services," Kendrick went on. "Most primitives don't like outsiders present at their ritual activities."

"Especially if there *are* actual manifestations of their god," Hammond contributed. "That would mean the priests are up to some sort of trickery, and they wouldn't care to run the risk of having us see through—"

He was interrupted by a loud crash from the kitchen.

"Are you all right, Iximi!" he yelled. "Need any help?"

"All is well!" she called back. "But, I pray you, do not enter, masters. The reverberation was part of a rite designed to deflect evil spirits from the food. Were a heretic to be present or interrupt the ceremonies, the spell would be voided and the food contaminated."

"Okay!" Peter returned and, in a lower tone, which he probably thought she could not overhear, "Seems you were right."

"Naturally." There was complacency in the professor's voice. "And now let us consider the validating features of the social structure as related to the mythos—and, of course, the ethos, where the two are not coincident—of the Uxenians...."

"Imagine," Zen complained in the kitchen, "accusing *Me* of being a mere trick of the priesthood—Supreme Me!"

"Supreme Butterfingers!" the princess snapped, irritation driving her to the point of sacrilege. "You spilled that red stuff, the ..." she bent over to read the legend on the container "... the ketchup all over the floor!"

"The floor is relatively clean," Zen murmured abstractedly. "We can scoop up the substance and incorporate it in whatever dainty dish we prepare for the Earthlings' repast. Now they'll think that I, Zen the Accessible, am difficult to have audience with," he mourned, "whereas I was particularly anxious to hold converse with them and discover what quest brings them to Uxen. That is," he added hastily, remembering he was omniscient, "just how they would justify its rationale."

"Shall we get on with our culinary activities, Almighty One?" Iximi asked coldly.

If the Most Fair and Exalted had a flaw, Zen thought, it was a one-track mind.

"What in hell did you put in this, Iximi?" Kendrick demanded, after one taste of the steaming casserole of food which she had set proudly before the two Earthmen.

"Ketchup, that's for sure...." Peter murmured, rolling a mouthful around his tongue as he sought to separate its component flavors. "And rhubarb, I should say."

"Dried fish and garlic...." Kendrick made further identifications.

"And a comestible called marshmallow," Iximi beamed. "You like it? I am *so* glad!"

"I do *not*—" Kendrick began, but Peter intervened.

"It's very nice, Iximi," he said tactfully, "but I guess we're just used to old run-of-the-mill Earth cooking. It's all our fault; we should have given you a recipe."

"I had a recipe," Iximi returned. "It came to me by Divine Inspiration."

Kendrick compressed his lips.

"Useful sort of divinity they have around here," Peter said. "Everything that goes wrong seems to take place in the name of religion. Are you sure you didn't happen to overhear us talking before, Iximi?"

"Don't be silly, Hammond!" Kendrick snapped. "These simple primitives do not have the sophistication to use their religious beliefs consciously as rationalization for their incompetence."

"Even had I wished to eavesdrop," Iximi said haughtily, "I would hardly have had the opportunity; I was too busy trying to prepare a palatable repast for you and—" her voice broke—"you didn't like it."

"Oh, I did like it, Iximi!" Peter protested. "It's just that I'm allergic to rhubarb."

"Wait!" she exclaimed, smiling again. "For dessert I have an especial surprise for you." She brought in a dish triumphantly. "Is this not just how you have it on Earth?"

"Stewed cigarettes with whipped cream," Kendrick muttered. "Stewed cigarettes! Where on Ear—on Uxen did you find them?"

"In a large box with the other puddings," she beamed. "Is it not highly succulent and flavorful?"

The two scientists sprang from their chairs and dashed into the kitchen. Iximi stared after them. When they returned, they looked much more cheerful. They seated themselves, and soon fragrant clouds of smoke began to curl toward the ceiling.

They are calling me at last, Zen thought happily, *and with such delightful incense! Who wants chants anyway?*

"But what are you *doing!*" the princess shrieked.

Zen hastened to manifest himself, complete with fourteen nostrils, before she could spoil everything. "The procedure is most unorthodox," he murmured aloud, "but truly this new incense has a most delicious aroma, extremely pleasing to My Ego. What is your will, oh, strangers?"

"All-Merciful Zen," the princess pleaded, "forgive them, for they knew not what they did. They did not mean to summon You."

"Then who," asked Zen in a terrible voice, "is this wonderful smoke for? Some foreign god whom they worship on My Territory?" And he wouldn't put it past them either.

Peter looked at the anthropologist, but Kendrick was obviously too paralyzed with fright to speak. "As a matter of fact, Your—er—Omnipotence," the physicist said haltingly, "this is not part of our religious ritual. We burn this particular type of incense which we call tobacco, for our own pleasure."

"In other words," Zen said coldly, "you worship yourselves. I work and slave My Godhood to the bone only to have egotists running all over My Planet."

"No, it's nothing like that at all," Kendrick quavered. "We smoke the tobacco to—well—gratify our appetites. Like—like eating, you know."

"Well, you will have to forego that pleasure," Zen said, frowning terribly. Even the tall one cowered, he noted with appreciation. It had been a long time since people had really cringed before his frown. The Uxenach had come to take him too much for granted; they would learn their mistake. "From now on," he said portentously, "the tobacco must be reserved for My Use alone. Smoke it only for purposes of worship. Once a day will be sufficient," he added graciously, "and perhaps twice on holy days."

"But we do not worship alien gods," Kendrick persisted in a shaky voice. "Even if you *were* a god...."

Zen frowned. "Would you care to step outside and test my divinity?"

"Well, no ... but...."

"Then, as far as you're concerned, I am Divine, and let's have no more quibbling. Don't forget the tobacco once a day. About time I had a change from that low-grade incense."

He vanished. Too late he remembered that he'd planned to ask the Earthlings why they had come to Uxen, and to discuss a little business proposition with them. Oh, well, time for that at his next materialization for them. And, now that he considered the matter, the direct approach might very well be a mistake.

He hoped Iximi would make sure they burned him tobacco regularly—really good stuff; almost made godhood worthwhile. But then he'd felt that way about incense at first. No, he had other ideas for making divinity worthwhile, and Iximi was going to help him, even if she didn't know it. People had used him long enough; it was his turn to use them.

In the kitchen, Iximi recalled Zen and together they washed the dishes and listened to the scientists quarreling in the next room.

"You will note the use of incense as standard socio-religious parallelism, Hammond. Men have appetites that must be gratified and so they feel their supreme being must also eat ... only, being a deity, he consumes aromas."

"Yes," Peter said. "You explained all that to Him much more succinctly, though."

"Hah! Well, have you any idea yet as to how the trick was worked?"

"Worked? What do you mean?"

"How they made that talking image appear? Clever device, I must say, although the Scoomps of Aldebaran III—"

"Didn't look like a trick to me."

"That's a fine young man," Zen said approvingly to Iximi. "I *like* him."

"You really do, Most High? I am *so* glad!"

"You don't mean you really believe this Zen is an actual living god?" Kendrick spluttered.

There was a silence. "No, not a god," Peter said finally, "but not a human, either. Perhaps another life-form with attributes different from ours. After all, do we know who or what was on Uxen, before it was colonized by Earth?"

"Tcha!" Kendrick said.

Iximi looked at Zen. Zen looked at Iximi. "The concept of godhood varies from society to society," the divinity told the princess. "Peter is not being sacrilegious, just manifesting a healthy skepticism."

"You're a credulous fool," Kendrick said hotly to his assistant. "I don't blame the Secretary for demoting you. When we return to Earth, I shall recommend your transfer to Refuse Removal. You have no business at all in Science!"

There was the sound of footsteps. "Leaving my noxious company?" Peter's voice asked tightly.

"I am going out to the nearest temple to have a chat with one of the priests. I can expect more sensible answers from him than from you!" The outside door slammed.

"Speaking of Refuse Removal, Almighty," Iximi said to Zen, "would you teleport the remains of this miserable repast to the Sacred Garbage Dump? And you need not return; I'll be able to handle the rest myself."

"Moolai Uxen," Zen reminded her and vanished with the garbage, but, although the refuse was duly teleported, the unseen, impalpable presence of the god remained.

The door to the kitchen opened, and Hammond walked in, his face grim. "Need any help, Iximi?" he asked, not very graciously. "Or should I say 'Your Royal Highness'?"

Iximi dropped a plate which, fortunately, was plastic. "How did you know who I was?"

He sat down on a stool. "Didn't you remember that your portrait hung in the great hall of the palace?"

"Of course," she said, chagrined. "A portrait of a servant would hardly be hung there."

"Not only that, but I asked whom it depicted. Do you think I wouldn't notice the picture of such a beautiful girl?"

"But if you knew, why then did you...?"

He grinned. "I realized you were up to no good, and I have no especial interest in the success of Kendrick's project."

Iximi carefully dried a dish. "And what is his project?"

"To investigate the mythos of the allegedly corporeal divinity in static primitive societies, with especial reference to the god-concept of Zen on Uxen."

"Is that *all*?"

All! Zen thought. *Sounds like an excellent subject for research to me. Unfortunate that I cannot possibly let the study be completed, as I am going to invalidate the available data very shortly.*

"That's all, Iximi."

"And how is it that Professor Kendrick did not recognize me from the picture?"

"Oh, he never notices girls' pictures. He's a complete idiot.... You overheard us just now? When we get back to Earth, I'm going to be a garbage collector."

"Here on Uxen, Refuse Removal is a Divine Prerogative," Iximi remarked.

"Poor Zen, whatever he is," Peter said to himself. "But a god, being a god," he went on in a louder voice, "can raise himself above the more sordid aspects of the job. As a mere human, I cannot, Iximi, I wonder if—" He looked nervously at his watch. "I hope Kendrick takes his time."

"He will not return soon," Iximi told him, putting away the dish towel. "Not if he is determined to find a temple. Because there are no temples. Zen is a god of the Hearth and Home."

"Iximi," Peter said, getting up and coming closer to her, "isn't there some way I can stay here on Uxen, some job I can fill? You're the crown princess—you must have a drag with the civil service." He looked at her longingly. "Oh, if only you weren't so far above me in rank."

"Listen, Peter!" She caught his hands. "If you were the Royal Physicist, our ranks would not be so far disparate. My distinguished father would make you a duke. And princesses have often ..." she blushed "... that is to say, dukes are considered quite eligible."

"Do you think I have a chance of becoming Royal Physicist?"

"I am certain of it." She came very close to him. "You could give us the atomic drive, design space ships ... weapons ... for us, couldn't you, darling?"

"I could." He looked troubled. "But it's one thing to become an extraterrestrial, another to betray my own world."

Iximi put her arms around him. "But Uxen will be your world, Peter. As prince consort, you would no longer be concerned with the welfare of the Earthlings."

"Yes, but...."

"And where is there betrayal? We do not seek to conquer Earth or its colonies. All we want is to regain our own freedom. We are entitled to freedom, aren't we, Peter?"

He nodded slowly. "I ... suppose so."

"Moolai Uxen." She thrust a package of cigarettes into his hand. "Let us summon the Almighty One to bless our betrothal."

Peter obediently lit two cigarettes and gave one to her.

Zen materialized his head. "Blessings on you, my children," he said, sniffing ecstatically, "and welcome, Holy Chief Physicist, to My Service."

"*Royal* Chief Physicist," Iximi corrected.

"No, that is insufficient for his merits. Holy and Sacrosanct Chief Physicist is what he will be, with the rank of prince. You will have the honor of serving Terrible Zen Myself, Peter Hammond."

"Delighted," said the young man dubiously.

"You will construct robots that do housework, vehicles that carry refuse to the Sacred Garbage Dump, vans that transport household goods, machines that lave dishes...."

"Will do," Peter said with obvious relief. "And may I say, Your—er—Benignness, that it will be a pleasure to serve You?"

"But the atomic power drive ... freedom?" Iximi stammered.

"These will point the surer, shorter way to the true freedom. My Omnidynamism has stood in the way of your cultural advancement, as Professor Kendrick will undoubtedly be delighted to explain to you."

"But, Your Omnipotence...."

"Let us have no more discussion. I am your God and I know best."

"Yes, Supreme One," Iximi said sullenly.

"You Uxenach have kept Me so busy for thousands of years, I have had no time for My Divine Meditations. I shall now withdraw Myself from mundane affairs."

The princess forgot disappointment in anxiety. "You will not leave us, Zen?"

"No, My child, I shall be always present, watching over My People, guiding them, ready to help them in case of emergency. But make sure I am not summoned save in case of dire need. No more baby-sitting, mind you."

"Yes, Almighty One."

"The incense will continue to be offered to me daily by everyone who seeks My Sacred Ear, and make sure to import a large quantity of this tobacco from Earth for holy days ... and other occasions," he added casually, "when you wish to be especially sure of incurring My Divine Favor. And I wish to be worshipped in temples like other gods." *Less chance of my being stuck with some unexpected household task.* "I shall manifest Myself on Thursdays only," he concluded gleefully, struck by the consummate idea. "Thursday will be My Day to work and your holy day. All other days you will work, and I will indulge in Divine Meditation. I have spoken."

And he withdrew all aspects of his personality to his retreat to wallow in the luxury of six days off per week. Naturally, to make sure the Uxenach kept the incense up to scratch, he would perform a small miracle now and again to show he was still Omnipresent.

Being a god, he thought as he made himself more comfortable, was not a bad thing at all. One merely needed to learn how to go about it in the right way.

Milton Keynes UK
Ingram Content Group UK Ltd.
UKHW030744071024
449371UK00006B/568